SHIRE NATURAL

G000162164

THE
SPARROWHAWK

IAN NEWTON

CONTENTS

Cover: *An adult male Sparrowhawk at a plucking post, Worcestershire.*

Series editor: Jim Flegg.

Published in 2001 by Shire Publications Ltd, Cromwell House, Church Street, Princes Risborough, Buckinghamshire HP27 9AA, UK.
Website: www.shirebooks.co.uk
Copyright © 1987 by Ian Newton.
First published 1987; reprinted 2001.
Number 16 in the Shire Natural History series. ISBN 0 85263 857 4.

Printed in Great Britain by CIT Printing Services Ltd, Press Buildings, Merlins Bridge, Haverfordwest, Pembrokeshire SA61 1XF.

Introduction

The Sparrowhawk *(Accipiter nisus)* is one of the commonest birds of prey in Europe, nesting in forest and woodland throughout the continent. It feeds almost entirely on other birds, especially small songbirds. Like other birds of prey, it has a hooked bill adapted for tearing flesh and sharp, curved claws for seizing and holding its quarry. Compared to most birds of prey, the Sparrowhawk is small, but it shows a remarkable divergence between the sexes. The larger female measures about 35 cm (14 inches) from head to tail and weighs around 300 grams (10 ounces) while the smaller male measures about 30 cm (12 inches) and weighs around 150 grams (5 ounces). In nearly all birds of prey the female is the bigger sex, but in the Sparrowhawk the difference is extreme. Linked with this, the sexes differ somewhat in their ecology — in habitat usage and in the range of prey taken.

Both sexes have a relatively slim body, long thin legs, short broad wings and a longish tail. This shape gives the birds great manoeuvrability and enables them to thread their way at speed through thick cover, twisting and turning to avoid obstacles. In both sexes the upper surface is bluish-grey and the underside is mainly whitish, with dark horizontal bars. The males also have some orange colouration on the chest and flanks. The juveniles are similar, except that all the parts which are blue-grey in the adults are brownish, and the underside lacks orange. The juvenile plumage lasts for the first year of life.

Despite its abundance, the Sparrowhawk is seldom seen. It spends most of its time in cover, and when in the open it flies fast and low, unnoticed by the human eye. Its usual flight consists of a short series of flaps, interspersed with long glides. The bird is usually seen as it skims along hedges or other lines of vegetation in search of prey, or when it makes a quick dash to seize some hapless victim from a garden bird table.

Many people confuse the Sparrowhawk with the similar-sized Kestrel *(Falco tinnunculus)*, which is commoner and much more often seen. It is the Kestrel which enlivens many a dull car journey as it perches on some telegraph post or hovers over some grassy patch in search of mice and voles. Both species are of similar size and have longish tails but, whereas the Kestrel has the long pointed wings of a falcon, the Sparrowhawk has the short broad wings of an accipiter. It is by their behaviour that they can best be distinguished, however, as a Kestrel can be watched for hours on end, whereas a Sparrowhawk is seldom glimpsed for more than a few seconds at a time.

Range and density

DISTRIBUTION

The Sparrowhawk has a wide geographical range, breeding in woods and forests across Europe and Asia, from Ireland east to Japan, and from the treeline in the north southwards into the Mediterranean region, including North Africa. The northernmost populations are migratory, and in winter the species reaches further south into desert scrub in Africa, the Middle East, India and southeast Asia, but it is not known to extend south of the equator. The Sparrowhawks that breed in Britain stay in the country all year, but in winter their numbers are swollen by migrants from Norway, Sweden and Finland. These northern birds arrive in September or October, spend the winter mainly in eastern districts, and leave again in March or April. Other migrants from Fennoscandia pass through eastern Britain each autumn and spring, as they travel to and from their wintering areas in the Low Countries, France and Spain. Their movements are known from ring recoveries.

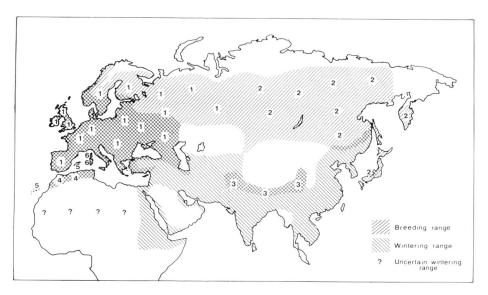

1. *The geographical range of the Sparrowhawk, showing breeding and wintering areas. The numbers relate to different races, as follows: 1 Accipiter nisus nisus, 2 A.n. nisosimilis, 3 A.n. melaschistos, 4 A.n. punicus, 5 A.n. granti, 6 A.n. wolterstorffi.*

2. *A Sparrowhawk nest (arrowed) in a willow thicket, Cumbria.*

HABITAT

Sparrowhawks generally require woodlands for nesting and roosting, but they hunt their prey almost anywhere, including all kinds of open country, sea coasts and gardens. In choice of nesting wood they show marked preferences, but in some localities they use sub-standard sites, if nothing better is available. Thus, they generally prefer large woods to small ones, but where large woods are scarce they nest readily in small woods, scrub patches or even small clumps of trees. Similarly, they prefer young, fairly thick, woods, with trees 2 to 4 metres (6 to 13 feet) apart, but will accept more open woods where necessary, including scattered trees in city parks. As nest trees, they prefer conifers, but where these are scarce they build readily in broad-leaved trees. The type of nesting habitat thus varies to some extent between districts, depending on what is available. Ideally, however, a nesting wood should offer plenty of cover, yet at the same time be open enough to permit easy flight between the trunks and branches. As long as a wood remains suitable, Sparrowhawks may nest there year after year, usually building a new nest each time in a tree near the old nests, forming a traditional nesting place, which is easily recognisable to the human observer. The nest itself is placed in the lower canopy, and the chosen tree is often near a stream, path or other opening, which provides the birds with easy access.

SPACING AND BREEDING DENSITY

The only way to discover what size of area a Sparrowhawk needs is to fix a small radio transmitter to it, so that it can be followed in its daily movements. Such work with radios has revealed that male Sparrowhawks distribute themselves in individual territories or 'home ranges', each of which contains a nesting place and hunting areas. In early spring, the home ranges of neighbouring males overlap little, but at other times of year they expand and overlap considerably. For most of the year females have much larger home ranges than males and their ranges overlap more. Thus, the home range of each female will normally include the ranges of two or more males and will overlap the ranges of several other females. In addition, the ranges of females extend more into open country than do those of males. At breeding time, however, each female settles on the nesting place of a particular male, and as she is fed by the male she can stay there and tend the nest. Only when the young are large enough to be left alone does the female begin to hunt again and travel away from the immediate nest area.

In extensive woodlands nesting places of different pairs tend to be regularly spaced, a reflection of the territorial behaviour of the males. In some districts such nesting places can be as close as 0.5 km (550 yards) to one another, but in other districts they can be more than 3 km (2 miles) apart. Their spacing depends on the food supply, as the hawks space themselves more widely, with larger home ranges, in districts where prey are scarce. As prey numbers are related to elevation and soil fertility, Sparrowhawk nesting places tend to be more widely spaced in woodland on high ground than on low, and on poorer than on richer soils.

Regular spacing is apparent only in well wooded areas. In more open country, with small woods, pairs are spaced according to the distribution of suitable woods, the distances between pairs being dictated largely by the distances between the woods. In districts with no woods breeding Sparrowhawks are usually absent. Thus, two factors can set a limit on breeding densities: in sparsely wooded terrain, as in most of Britain, breeding numbers are limited by shortage of nesting places (woods), whereas in well wooded terrain, where nesting places are superabundant, numbers are limited instead by food supply. These factors provide only an upper limit on breeding numbers, which may often fall below this level under the influence of other factors, such as persecution or pesticides.

In various districts of Britain, densities of 14 to 96 Sparrowhawk pairs per 100 square kilometres (39 square miles) have been found, depending largely on the ratio of wooded to open terrain. Extrapolating from these figures, the maximum likely Sparrowhawk population in

3. *An adult female at the nest with her young, Surrey.*

4. *An adult female feeding her young, Dumfriesshire.*

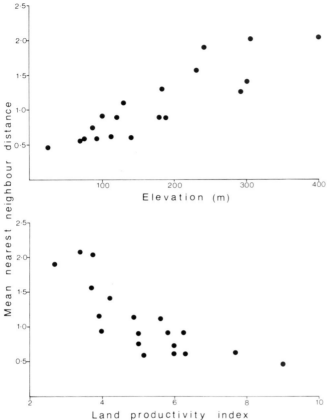

5. *Sparrowhawk nest spacing in continuous woodland, shown in relation to elevation above sea level and land fertility, in different parts of Britain. Sparrowhawks nest further apart (at lower density) with an increase in elevation and a decrease in land fertility.*

the whole of Britain, excluding Ireland, is probably around 32,000 pairs, as well as a large but unknown number of non-breeders.

In any one district Sparrowhawk populations usually remain fairly stable over long periods, with only minor changes in nest numbers between years. This was known to early naturalists and egg collectors, who could usually rely on finding nests in the same places year after year, with only occasional absences. More recent research in particular areas has tended to confirm this. Providing the land use remains stable and the area of woodland does not change greatly, nest numbers normally fluctuate within about 10 to 15 per cent of the mean over long

periods of years. Compared to the fluctuations which are theoretically possible, this represents a remarkable degree of stability. It presumably comes about because the food supply of Sparrowhawks is itself relatively stable. Feeding on a wide range of bird species, the hawks are buffered against a temporary shortage of any one species, so can maintain their numbers from year to year. In contrast, Kestrels in most districts have restricted diets, based on voles. These small rodents fluctuate greatly in abundance from year to year, often in regular three to five year cycles, and promote similar fluctuations in the numbers of their predators, including Kestrels.

6

Feeding habits

The Sparrowhawk is the only woodland bird of prey in Europe which specialises in taking small birds. Its foraging behaviour is difficult to study, because most hunting occurs among trees and bushes, and the individual prey captures occupy no more than a moment, so are easily missed. To catch its prey, a Sparrowhawk has the benefit of a keen eye, great stealth and manoeuvrability, but it is not especially fast in level flight. The usual speed is 30 to 40 km per hour (20 to 25 mph), reaching 50 km per hour (30 mph) in short bursts. The hawk is thus somewhat faster than most songbirds, which fly at less than 35 km per hour (22 mph), but slower than Swallows, waders and larger prey, such as pigeons. For its size, a Sparrowhawk can twist and turn with remarkable ease, but smaller birds can still outmanoeuvre it. To avoid an attacking hawk, small birds normally flee into thick cover, but larger and faster birds take to the air. Some flocking species in open country bunch together and perform fast zigzag flights which prevent the hawk from singling out a victim.

Radio-tracking individual hawks has revealed that they hunt mainly by ambush, using cover to gain a close approach, and then moving in for a short, swift attack. In such attacks the prey usually notices the hawk approaching and makes straight for the nearest cover, so the hawk has only a few seconds in which to grab its victim. Most prey are seized while they are still perched or just after they have taken flight. In the commonest method of hunting, called 'short-stay perch-hunting', the hawk makes a series of short flights through woodland or from one patch of cover to the next, pausing for a few minutes to scan the surroundings, and then passing on to the next perch to search again. It usually sits well inside a tree in order to stay hidden. Alternatively, the bird may fly along hedges or other lines of vegetation, continually flipping from one side to the other, in the hope of surprising a victim. The hawk has several other hunting techniques, including sitting and waiting at strategic points, or even stooping on prey from a great height, but these are used much less commonly. The salient feature of most of the Sparrowhawk's hunting is self-concealment, to which end the hawk usually flies close to the ground and takes advantage of any cover or irregularity in terrain to gain a hidden approach.

Small prey is probably killed by the impact of capture or by being squeezed in the hawk's foot. Nonetheless, some birds are not killed in this way and if the victim persists in struggling the hawk will continue to squeeze it, opening and closing its grip on the body, which is repeatedly punctured by the claws. Otherwise, Sparrowhawks have no special behaviour for killing large prey. They seem merely to attempt to bring the victim to ground, hold it down and start eating. The long legs of the hawk enable the prey to be held away from the body, which is an advantage in dealing with thrashing wings or jabbing bill. By these actions Sparrowhawks are able to subdue prey larger than they can carry or eat in one meal.

The hawk normally plucks its prey on a stump, log or other low mound, or occasionally on a horizontal branch or old nest in a tree. The hawk stands on its victim to hold it down, and removes the feathers with its bill. On the ground, the site of action often appears afterwards as a circle of feathers, around where the hawk stood. From small prey the hawk eats all parts of the carcase — bones, guts and all — and leaves only the feathers. But from large birds it often leaves bill, legs or other parts which are difficult to break up and swallow. Once in the hawk's digestive tract the bones cause no further problem, as they can be readily digested.

Almost any bird species of appropriate size is fair game. As the female Sparrowhawk is bigger than the male, she can tackle larger prey. The male eats mainly small, sparrow-sized birds, occasionally taking species up to the size of Blackbird or Mistle Thrush, whereas the female eats mainly thrush-sized birds but occasionally takes species up to the size of full-grown Wood Pigeons. The exact composition of the diet depends largely on what is available locally, but within

6. *The head of a female Sparrowhawk.*
7. *A first-year female at her nest.*

this range certain species are more vulnerable to Sparrowhawk attack than others. Conspicuous species which feed away from cover, such as the Chaffinch, are highly vulnerable, whereas skulking species which seldom leave cover, such as the Wren, are taken much less than would be expected from their numbers. In much of Britain common songbirds, such as the Chaffinch, House Sparrow, Blackbird, Song Thrush and Starling, predominate in the diet, with the addition of Redwing and Fieldfare in winter.

Although birds make up the bulk of the food, small mammals are eaten occasionally. These include mainly voles and mice, but also young rabbits or even bats. Also, while most of the prey are taken live, Sparrowhawks occasionally eat birds and mammals which they find already dead. Females seem to take more mammals and more carrion than do males. The average food consumption has been measured at around 40 to 50 grams (1.4 to 1.8 ounces) per day for males and 50 to 70 grams (1.8 to 2.5 ounces) per day for the larger females, depending partly on their activity. The number of carcases needed to provide this ration varies with their size, but it is equivalent to about two and three sparrows per day respectively for each sex. Over a whole year total food intake amounts to around 16.5 kg (36 pounds) of meat for a male and 22 kg (48 pounds) for a female. Added to the needs of breeding, a successful Sparrowhawk pair could account for 55 kg (121 pounds) of meat in a year. This is equivalent to about 2200 House Sparrows, or 600 Blackbirds, or 110 Wood Pigeons.

Despite this heavy predation, Sparrowhawks are not known to have any long-term effect on the breeding numbers of their prey species. During the 1960s Sparrowhawks were largely absent from most of Britain, having been poisoned by organochlorine pesticides (see below). From counts in the breeding season, no great upsurge in songbird prey populations occurred then, and similarly no decline in such populations was noted in the 1970s when Sparrowhawks returned. The main effect of Sparrowhawks on

8. *The remains of a Wood Pigeon plucked and eaten by a Sparrowhawk.*

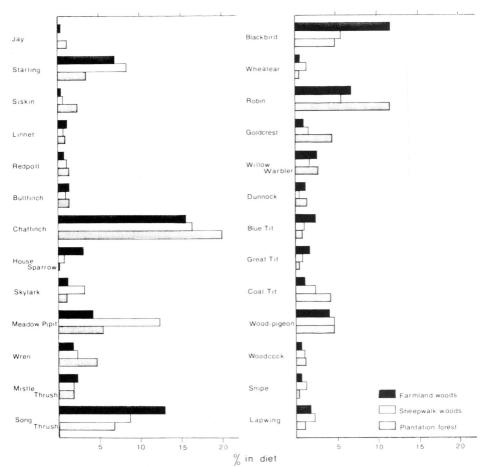

9. *The diet of Sparrowhawks during the breeding season in different habitats in south Scotland.*
Only prey species which formed at least one per cent of the diet are shown; other species were taken,
but in smaller numbers. (From Newton, 1986.)

their prey is to alter the seasonal pattern of mortality and reduce the numbers of prey dying from other causes. Thus, instead of dying mainly in winter from food shortage, in the presence of Sparrowhawks songbirds die at all times of the year, mainly from predation.

In the past many Sparrowhawks were shot because of their depredations on game birds. This was when Pheasant chicks were raised under broody hens in coops set in open fields. In these conditions the chicks were extremely vulner-able and were regularly attacked by Sparrowhawks, so the gamekeeper had legitimate complaint. Nowadays, most Pheasants are raised indoors under heat-producing lamps, and by the time the young birds are put in pens in the woods they are already grown beyond the favoured size range of prey. Consequent-ly extremely few are taken. Predation by Sparrowhawks on other game species is negligible, but full-grown Partridges have occasionally been recorded in the diet of females.

10

RELATIONSHIP WITH THE GOSHAWK

The Sparrowhawk belongs to one of the largest groups of raptors, forming the genus *Accipiter,* which contains about fifty species occupying forest and scrub habitats throughout the world. Over most of Europe it breeds alongside its larger relative the Goshawk *(Accipiter gentilis).* Together, the two species form a graded size series, from male and female Sparrowhawk to male and female Goshawk. Between them these four sizes of accipiters exploit as food almost the entire bird population of wooded parts of their range, excluding only the very largest species. All of them can kill prey heavier than themselves, but the Goshawk eats larger prey, including more mammals than the Sparrowhawk. It also nests in more mature, more open forest, and thus differs both in diet and in habitat from the smaller species. The Goshawk is also the main natural predator of the Sparrowhawk, taking adult birds, together with nestlings and fledglings which have recently left the nest. It was exterminated in Britain during the nineteenth century but has re-established itself in some regions, as a result of escapes of falconry birds imported from the continent.

10. *A Goshawk at its nest with its young. Much larger than the Sparrowhawk, the Goshawk typically nests in more mature woodland and takes larger prey species. It is also the main natural predator of the Sparrowhawk.*

11. *A first-year male Sparrowhawk at a plucking post with its prey.*

12. *An adult female incubating at a nest in a pine, Worcestershire.*

13. *An adult female feeding small chicks, Dumfriesshire.*

14. *An adult female dismembering a freshly plucked songbird for its young, Dumfriesshire.*

The breeding season

Sparrowhawks breed in summer, when their food is most readily available. At this season the songbird prey are themselves breeding, so there are many vulnerable fledglings for Sparrowhawks to eat. Such young birds, which have just left the nest, provide especially easy pickings, because they cannot fly properly and they attract attention to themselves by calling for food. The Sparrowhawk breeding season coincides almost exactly with the period when fledgling songbirds are available, and the hawks continually switch emphasis from one prey species to another, as each produces its young. In most years the first hawks to lay eggs start within five to ten days after the earliest fledglings appear in their diets. And the period of peak food demand, when the majority of hawks have young, coincides with the period of peak fledgling supply, mid June to mid July.

In early spring Sparrowhawks re-establish themselves on nesting places in preparation for breeding. This period is characterised by nest building, displays and other interactions between the pair, and the provision of food from male to female. The males, already established on their territories, are visited by females which compete with one another for the opportunity to breed. Once a female settles on a nesting place with a male, her initial function is to ward off other females. Special flight displays are used as warnings to signal occupancy of a nesting place, and these occasionally escalate to chases and fights. The warning displays take place high above the nesting place and are easy to recognise. Typically a bird will suddenly swing upwards for 20 metres (65 feet) or more, then gently tip forward, close its wings and dive downwards. At the bottom of the dive it opens its wings and swings upwards again to repeat the performance, making a series of U-shaped undulations in the airspace. For a bird which usually remains hidden below the canopy, these undulating displays in the open are very conspicuous. They usually seem to be given in response to another bird in the air, and if the intruder does not leave it may be chased away or fought in foot-to-foot combat. Within the wood itself, females also chase intruders from the nesting place, calling loudly, with a strident 'kek... kek...kek...'.

Other displays above the nesting wood involve the pair soaring together, first one and then the other uppermost, and

15. *The annual cycle of the Sparrowhawk in Britain, showing the timing of various stages of breeding, moult and dispersal.*

	Jan	Feb	Mar	Apr	May	Jun	Jul	Aug	Sep	Oct	Nov	Dec
Nest-building												
Egg-laying												
Incubating												
Feeding young in nest												
Feeding young out of nest												
Young dispersing												
Adult males moulting												
Adult females moulting												

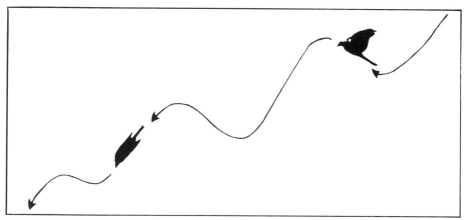

16. *The undulating flight display of the Sparrowhawk, used in advertisement and defence of the nesting place.*

occasional diving displays by the male as he stoops past the female into the trees. As the time of egg laying approaches, copulations also become frequent and may occur several times each morning. They usually take place on a branch near the nest.

To feed the hen, the cock brings prey to the nest vicinity, one item at a time, and calls to the hen with a soft 'kew... kew...kew...'. Usually he has already plucked the prey, but otherwise he may pluck it in full view of the hen, with exaggerated movements. The hen takes the item from him, either on a perch or in the air, in a foot-to-foot pass. This behaviour is commonly called courtship feeding, but it continues for much of the breeding cycle and well beyond the courtship phase. It is initially important in enabling the hen to accumulate the body reserves necessary for egg production. Some days before egg laying, the hen becomes wholly dependent on the male for food, if she is not already, and may then receive several meals each day.

The nest, which is made of twigs, may be started as early as January, but usually not until March or April in preparation for eggs in May. Both sexes help to build, but the male makes most of the initial structure, while the female does the lining. The completed nest is a fairly flat, bulky structure. It is usually about 40 to 80 cm (16 to 32 inches) across and 10 to 30 cm (4 to 12 inches) deep, while the central cup is about 15 to 20 cm (6 to 8 inches) across and 5 to 10 cm (2 to 4 inches) deep. The whole structure weighs around 1 to 2 kg (2 to 4 pounds) and may contain up to 1500 twigs. It is usually lined with fine twigs or flakes of bark. The twigs are broken from trees nearby, and as they are carried and positioned one at a time nest building takes a lot of time and energy. The function of the nest is to provide a safe and stable platform for the eggs and young. Its position low in the canopy makes it hard to see from both above and below. This gives it some protection, but not complete protection, from predators which eat eggs or chicks.

Although most Sparrowhawks in Britain start egg laying in May, some begin in late April and others in early June. If the first clutch is taken and a replacement is laid, this can be started as late as mid June, at least in southern England. As a result, egg laying in the population may be spread over a six or seven week period. Most clutches contain four to six eggs (range one to seven), and no more than one brood is raised in a year.

The eggs are very attractive. They are basically pale blue or pale green, more or less covered with red-brown blotches and spots of various shapes, sizes and intensities. Marking varies greatly, and no two eggs look alike. The markings help to break up the outline of the eggs and

15

17. *A female attempting to shelter a chick in pouring rain, Dumfriesshire.*

18. *A first-year female at her nest in a birch wood, Surrey.*

19. *A brood of young ready to leave the nest. An addled egg remains.*

20. *An adult female with feathered young, Surrey.*

21. *Sparrowhawk eggs have a pale blue background, with red-brown marks. However, they vary greatly and no two eggs look alike, even in the same clutch. These are eggs from different clutches and show some of the variation.*

make them difficult for a predator to see. In the dappled sunlight of the tree tops the eggs are remarkably well camouflaged. Within a clutch, the eggs are laid on alternate days, and incubation normally begins with the penultimate egg, so that the hatch is spread over several days. The hen does all the incubating, and during this time she is provided with food by the male. She eats each meal on a nearby perch and returns immediately to the nest. If the cock cannot supply enough food, forcing the hen to hunt for herself, the eggs are then left exposed to predators, such as Jays or squirrels.

If all goes well, the eggs hatch after 32 to 34 days of incubation. The newly hatched chicks have a complete covering of white down. From the start they can open their eyes and take food morsels directly from their mother's bill. When the cock brings food, the hen takes the item (already plucked) to the nest and tears off tiny morsels, offering them to the young, one at a time. If the young cannot eat all the prey at one meal, the hen either finishes it herself or caches it nearby for a later meal.

When the chicks are small the hen stays at the nest and the cock does all the hunting, but when the young are larger the hen hunts too. The hen also broods the young, protects them from rain, sun and predators, divides prey for them and keeps the nest clear of prey remains. The young are brooded almost continuously for the first seven or eight days, then progressively less until twelve to fifteen days, and thereafter chiefly during rain. On average the young receive about eight meals per day, but this varies from one day to the next and from one brood to another.

The young grow quickly: the females gain weight more rapidly, but the males develop more quickly in other respects

18

and are able to fly at twenty-six days, compared with thirty days in the females. The faster development of the males may help them to survive in the presence of larger sisters. In some nests chicks may die from starvation, and at a later stage, when the parents are away hunting, young may die from chilling during rain storms or from predation. The main predators of well grown young are Tawny Owls, Goshawks and Pine Martens, but occasionally young are taken by other Sparrowhawks to feed their own broods.

Because males are smaller than females, it used to be thought that when food was scarce male chicks would lose in competition, leading to a surplus of females among fledglings. This is not the case, however, for as nestlings starve the last hatched is usually first to die, followed by the second last, and so on, irrespective of their sex. In consequence, the overall sex ratio at fledging is equal, but not necessarily in individual broods. In sex composition, Sparrowhawk broods do not differ from human families: any ratio is possible within broods, but in the population as a whole, males equal females.

Once the young have left the nest, they remain in the vicinity for another three or four weeks, fed by their parents. During this period the young complete their growth and develop the flying skills necessary to catch prey. At the end of this period the young disperse, and from then on they have to feed themselves.

Many pairs fail to rear young. Of 1400 nests found in south Scotland during 1971-84, 15 per cent were abandoned before egg laying. Of the nests which contained eggs, 28 per cent failed before hatching, and of those which hatched successfully a further 7 per cent failed before fledging. So, in total, 44 per cent of nests, or 33 per cent of clutches, produced no fledglings. Successful nests produced an average of 3.4 young, which was equivalent to 2.3 young per clutch laid, or to 1.9 young per nest built. This last figure gave the best estimate of overall breeding success, because it took account of failures at all stages from nest building onwards. Besides failure to lay eggs, the main causes of nest disaster included the desertion of clutches and

egg breakage due to pesticide contamination (see below). Minor causes included nest collapse, tree felling, persecution by humans, and predation or starvation of young. Several of the major causes, including non-laying and clutch desertion, were ultimately caused by food shortage.

Because the main natural predators of the Sparrowhawk, namely the Goshawk and the Pine Marten, are scarce or absent over most of Britain, natural predation rates may be lower than would otherwise occur. On the other hand, failures from pesticide contamination are a recent phenomenon, dating from the introduction of DDT in 1947.

22. *Causes of nest failure among Sparrowhawks in south Scotland, 1971-84. Results are expressed (upper) as a percentage of all nests found (total 1389) and (lower) as a percentage of all failures (total 606). N — natural failures, P — failures associated with pesticide contamination, H — failures due to direct human intervention. (From Newton, 1986.)*

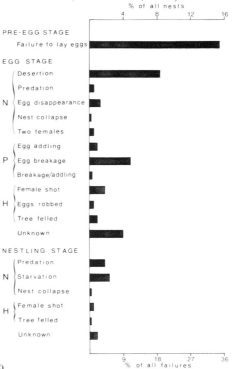

Some Sparrowhawks start breeding in their first year of life, while they are still in brown juvenile plumage, but the majority wait until their second, third or even fourth year. This is because food or nesting places are often in short supply, and old birds take precedence over young ones. In addition, certain individuals which have bred previously sometimes have a non-breeding year. On average, only about half the females in a population may build nests in any one year. The amount of non-breeding among males is probably less, because most populations contain fewer males than females. As Sparrowhawks are normally monogamous, there are always some surplus females which cannot breed.

To some extent mating is selective with respect to age (and plumage colour). More yearling-yearling and more adult-adult pairs occur, and fewer adult-yearling pairs, than expected if mating were entirely random between these age groups. On average adult-adult pairs produce most young, and yearling-yearling pairs produce fewest, while mixed-aged pairs are intermediate. Age of both cock and hen has some influence on the number of young produced and this is most plausibly explained as an effect of experience, as older birds are more skilled at catching prey. Perhaps, therefore, birds of both age groups prefer to mate with adult partners and accept yearlings only when they have no choice.

Most Sparrowhawks have a different mate each year and relatively few pairs remain intact from year to year. This is partly because of high mortality (about one-third die each year) and partly because of movements, as some birds change territories from one year to the next. Change of territory entails a change of mate, even if the mate of the previous year is still alive. In any one district, the available territories tend to vary in quality (food supply). The good territories are much in demand and, in general, individuals tend to move from poor to good territories during the course of their lives. Once they get a good territory, birds normally stay there but, with a high mortality, this is seldom more than a year or two. So although some Sparrowhawk territories are occupied for periods of fifty years or more, this results from many different individuals occupying such territories in quick succession, mostly for short periods of one or two years. Extreme residence periods recorded in south Scotland were four years for a male and six for a female.

MOULT

Like many other birds, Sparrowhawks replace their plumage once each year. Their moult takes about four months and overlaps extensively with breeding. Most females begin in May, around the time of egg laying, and most males begin in June, around the time of hatch. Both sexes continue into September or October, well beyond the date in August when their young become independent. However, many individuals stop moulting for a period in mid June to mid August, while they are feeding large young.

The moult occurs in summer, probably because this is the season when prey are most available, and when the hawks can best afford the reduction in flying ability caused by missing feathers. The later start of moult in cocks enables them to retain full-wing efficiency at a time when food supply has still not reached its peak and when they have to provision their incubating mates. Arrested moult in both sexes gives them full-wing efficiency at a time when the food demands of their young are greatest. In these ways the conflicting needs of moult and breeding are partly reconciled.

The moult is a demanding process because the feathers consist of keratins, which are proteins containing sulphur-amino-acids. These are scarce in other tissues, so the hawk has to consume more protein than normal just to get enough of these sulphur compounds. In addition, feather growth requires extra energy and results in greater heat loss than normal. In these respects Sparrowhawks are no different from other birds.

DISPERSAL

Although British Sparrowhawks are non-migratory, individuals disperse from the immediate nest area once they become independent and soon settle in their future breeding area. Most information

23. *A female Sparrowhawk bathing, Worcestershire.*

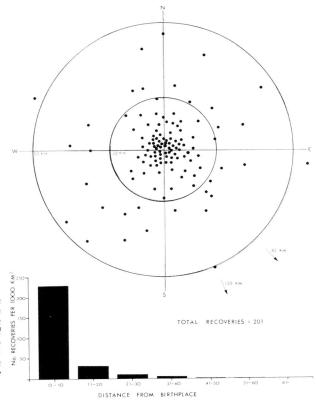

24. *The dispersal of British Sparrowhawks. (Upper) Each spot indicates a breeding season recovery of a ringed individual shown in relation to its birthplace (the centre). (Lower) Density of recoveries in successive circles out from the birthplace. (From Newton, 1986.)*

21

on the distances they move between their natal and subsequent breeding place comes from the recoveries of ringed individuals. Young birds are ringed in the nest by qualified ornithologists, and they are reported later in life when found by other people. About three-quarters of all Sparrowhawks recovered in Britain up to 1972 were within 20 km (12 miles) of their birthplace, and only a minority were beyond 50 km (30 miles). The furthest had moved about 300 km (190 miles). Recoveries came from all points of the compass, indicating no directional preference. This applied even to members of the same brood, which sometimes went in opposite directions. No evidence was found for any substantial movement in winter, even in hard years.

An interesting feature of this post-fledging dispersal is that, in general, females move further than males. This holds even with brothers and sisters from the same nest. The same occurs in some other bird species, including other raptors, and it may serve to reduce the chance of inbreeding. If one sex moves further than the other, close relatives have little chance of pairing together, as males are most likely to encounter females from more distant areas.

As dispersal occurs every year, with each crop of young, it serves to mix the individuals from different broods and from different localities. It also helps to redistribute the population, as individuals can leave districts where numbers are already high and settle where numbers are depleted. Once the birds have bred, they tend to stay in the same district for the rest of their lives, but not necessarily on the same nesting territories. Birds which change territories do not normally move far, perhaps to a neighbouring wood. Together with mortality, the changes of territory result in about a 50 per cent turnover in the individuals on particular territories from year to year.

Mortality

Compared with some other birds of prey, Sparrowhawks are short-lived, and a substantial part of the population dies each year. In their population dynamics Sparrowhawks do not differ greatly from the small songbirds which form their prey. Information on mortality rates comes from studies of ringed birds, mostly found and reported by members of the public. On this basis, the average mortality over the first year of life has been estimated at 69 per cent for cocks and 51 per cent for hens. In other words, many fewer cocks than hens survive their first year. In later life the death rate is lower and more similar between the sexes, at 33 per cent per year for cocks and 29 per cent per year for hens. These are average figures for all birds more than one year old. Almost all cocks are dead before they can reach eight years, and almost all hens before they can reach ten. As the sex ratio at fledging is equal, it is this greater mortality in males which leads to a surplus of females among birds of breeding age.

The greater mortality of males is hard to explain but, being smaller, they are less able to withstand food shortage than females and may also be more vulnerable to predation. Some males are even killed by female Sparrowhawks, for which they make an ideal-sized prey item. The difference in first-year mortality occurs mainly in August and September, in the first two months of independent life, when weights suggest that many more young males than young females die of starvation. As prey are plentiful in the countryside then, the starvation of young hawks is presumably due to their inexperience.

A second main period of starvation, which affects adults as well as juveniles, occurs in early spring, when prey are at their scarcest. At this time, just before breeding, the numbers of resident prey species reach their lowest level of the year, most winter migrants have left Britain and most summer migrants have not yet arrived. So it is not surprising that many Sparrowhawks die then.

While starvation is probably the main natural cause of death among Sparrowhawks, some die from human-related causes. These include shooting by gamekeepers and accidents, through hitting windows or wires. Most ring recoveries are from birds which have died from collisions of one sort or another and hence fallen into human hands. The proportion of birds recovered against windows has increased greatly in recent years, with the rise in popularity of plate glass and 'see-through' houses. So has the proportion killed by road vehicles increased as the volume of fast traffic has risen. On the other hand, the proportion reported as shot has declined in recent years, with the onset of protective legislation and a more benevolent attitude towards the species. Ring recoveries do not reflect the true pattern of mortality, as birds dying from certain causes are more likely to be found than are others. A hawk which crashes through a kitchen window will be noticed, whereas one eaten by a predator in some remote forest will probably not.

EFFECTS OF PESTICIDES

Sparrowhawks are unusual among birds in the extent to which their populations have been affected by agricultural pesticides. Not all kinds of pesticides are involved, but chiefly the organochlorine compounds, which include DDT, as well as aldrin, dieldrin and others. These pesticides are important because they are chemically very stable, so that they persist in the environment for long periods of years. They are highly soluble in fat and therefore they can accumulate in animal bodies and pass from prey to predator. So species, such as the Sparrowhawk, which are near the tops of food chains, are especially likely to take in large amounts with their food. Furthermore, as organochlorines can be transported in the bodies of animals, including migrant birds, they can affect Sparrowhawks in areas remote from agriculture.

During the 1950s and 1960s the organochlorine pesticides caused a massive decline in Sparrowhawk populations throughout Europe. In Britain the species almost disappeared from eastern districts, with intense arable agriculture, and became much reduced elsewhere. Similar declines were noted in some other birds of prey, especially in the Peregrine (*Falco peregrinus*) and Merlin (*F. columbarius*). Like the Sparrowhawk, these two falcons eat birds. Compared to some other animals, birds have a very poor ability to break down organochlorine pesticides in their bodies. Residues therefore build up more rapidly in birds than in other animals, making predators of birds all the more likely to accumulate dangerous amounts.

The different types of organochlorines have different effects on birds of prey. DDT is converted in the bird's body to DDE, which causes eggshell thinning, in turn leading to egg breakage and embryo deaths, and hence to reduced breeding output. In some areas of heavy DDT use, this reduction in breeding output was probably sufficient on its own to cause some decline in Sparrowhawk populations. The birds produce insufficient young to offset the normal mortality, so that numbers decline. Aldrin and dieldrin are much more toxic than DDT and cause deaths of adult birds. It was through this extra mortality, superimposed on poor breeding, that populations over much of Britain declined. This was evident from the speed of the decline, which took only one or two years in the worst affected areas, and from the finding of many dead Sparrowhawks with lethal burdens of dieldrin in their bodies. Recovery in populations followed successive restrictions in the use of aldrin, dieldrin and DDT on farmland, mainly in 1962, 1965, 1975 and 1986. The recovery took place in a wave-like pattern, west to east, occurring first in areas with least pesticide use (and least marked decline). By about 1992 the recovery was effectively complete and even the most intensively arable areas of south-east England had been re-colonised. The same was true over the rest of western Europe.

Some organo-mercury compounds are the only other pesticides known to have killed large numbers of Sparrowhawks and other predators. In the 1950s, these chemicals were used as fungicides on cereal seed and were studied mainly in Sweden. Like the organochlorines, these mercury compounds were very persistent and could pass from prey to predator, accumulating to lethal levels.

As a result of the problems caused by persistent pesticides, the emphasis in more recent years has been on less persistent types, which break down quickly to harmless residues. We owe a lot to the Sparrowhawk and other predators for providing us with an early warning system for chemicals which might have had serious effects on people, had their use continued.

THE FUTURE

Apart from a residual pesticide problem, the future for the Sparrowhawk in Britain looks good. Increasing afforestation of the uplands is providing extra breeding habitat in areas which formerly lacked it. This is enabling the birds to extend their breeding distribution. In addition, with a more tolerant human attitude, Sparrowhawks are gradually colonising many cities, including Edinburgh and London. In Edinburgh the birds were first found nesting in 1980, and five years later had increased to around forty pairs, breeding in such sites as parks and cemeteries. The cities of Britain could hold substantial numbers of Sparrowhawks, so that, if the colonisation continues, these dashing predators could well become familiar to a far wider range of people. The only factor acting against Sparrowhawks is the decline in farmland birds, potentially important prey, caused by intensive farming methods. This could in turn reduce Sparrowhawk numbers, however good are the other aspects of habitat.

Further reading

Cramp, S., and Simmons, K.E.L. (editors). *Handbook of the Birds of Europe, the Middle East and North Africa,* volume 2. Oxford University Press, 1980.

Newton, Ian. *The Sparrowhawk.* T. & A. D. Poyser, 1986.

Newton, I., and Haas, M.B. 'The Return of the Sparrowhawk', *British Birds,* volume 77, number 2, 1984.

Newton, I. 'Lifetime Reproductive Output of Female Sparrowhawks', *Journal of Animal Ecology,* volume 54, pages 241–53, 1989.

Newton, I. 'Habitat Variation and Population Regulation in Sparrowhawks', *Ibis,* volume 33, supplement 1, pages 76–88.

Wyllie, I., and Newton, I. 'Demography of an Increasing Population of Sparrowhawks', *Journal of Animal Ecology,* volume 60, pages 749–66, 1991.

ACKNOWLEDGEMENTS

The author wishes to thank Mrs M. B. Haas and Mr N. J. Westwood for help with the illustrations. Photographs are acknowledged to: W. Alston, 7, 18; R. J. C. Blewitt, cover and 10, 12, 23; D. A. Ratcliffe, 2; N. J. Westwood, 3, 20, 21; J. F. Young, 4, 11, 13, 14, 17, 19. The remaining photographs are by the author.